S0-BRU-956

DISCARDED

GREAT HEROES

ANN WEIL

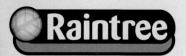
Raintree

Chicago, Illinois

Public Library
Incorporated 1882
Barrie, Ontario

© 2007 Raintree
a division of Reed Elsevier Inc.
Chicago, Illinois

Customer Service   888-363-4266

Visit our website at www.heinemannraintree.com

All rights reserved. No part of this publication
may be reproduced or transmitted in any form or
by any means, electronic or mechanical, including
photocopying, recording, taping, or any information
storage and retrieval system, without permission in
writing from the publisher.

Photo research by Hannah Taylor and Sally Claxton
Designed by Victoria Bevan and Bigtop
Printed in China by WKT

11 10 09 08 07
10 9 8 7 6 5 4 3 2 1

**Library of Congress Cataloging-in-Publication
Data**

Weil, Ann.
   Great heroes / Ann Weil.
      p. cm. -- (Atomic)
   Includes bibliographical references and index.
   ISBN 1-4109-2483-1 (lib bdg. : hardcover) --
ISBN 1-4109-2488-2 (pbk.)
   1. Heroes--Biography--Juvenile literature. 2.
Courage--Juvenile literature.
  I. Title. II. Series: Atomic (Chicago, Ill.)
  CT1059.W45 2006
  920.073--dc22

      2006000230

Acknowledgments
The author and publisher are grateful to the
following for permission to reproduce copyright
material: pp. **14–15**, Alamy Images/ Thorsten Eckert;
p. **10**, Corbis; p. **18**, Corbis Sygma/Jerry Ohlinger;
pp. **20–21**, Corbis/ David Pu'u; pp. **4–5**, Corbis/
George Hall; p. **4**, Corbis/Bettmann; pp. **24–25**,
Corbis/James Leynse; p. **9** bot, Corbis/Marianna
Day-Massey/ZUMA; p. **13**, Corbis/Neville Elder;
pp. **6–7**, Corbis/Paul A Souders; p. **19**, Corbis/
Reuters/Christian Charisius; pp. **8–9**, Corbis/Tim de
Waele; pp. **22–23**, Empics/Aislinn Simpson/PA; p. **14**
bot, Empics/Richard Drew/AP; p. **16**, Empics/Vincent
Laforet/AP; p. **26**, FLPA/ Minden Pictures/ Norbert
Wu; p. **29**, Free the Children.

Cover image of Lance Armstrong reproduced with
permission from Getty Images/ Robert Laberge.

The publisher would like to thank Nancy Harris,
Diana Bentley, and Dee Reid for their assistance in
the preparation of this book.

Every effort has been made to contact copyright
holders of any material reproduced in this book. Any
omissions will be rectified in subsequent printings if
notice is given to the publisher.

Disclaimer
All the Internet addresses (URLs) given in this book
were valid at the time of going to press. However,
due to the dynamic nature of the Internet, some
addresses may have changed, or sites may have
changed or ceased to exist since publication. While
the author and publishers regret any inconvenience
this may cause readers, no responsibility for any
such changes can be accepted by either the author
or the publishers.

Contents

Some words are printed in bold, **like this**. You can find out what they mean in the glossary. You can also look in the box at the bottom of the page where the word first appears.

WHAT IS A HERO?

There are many kinds of heroes. Some heroes are famous. Other heroes are ordinary people. Animals can be heroes, too.

A hero is brave

"What's a hero? I didn't even think about it," said Uli Derickson. She worked on a plane that was **hijacked** in 1985. Everyone on board was in great danger.

Derickson **persuaded** the hijackers to let some passengers go free. The hijackers warned they would kill people unless the plane got more gas. Derickson paid for the gas with her own credit card!

Derickson (center) won the Silver Cross award for valor.

hijack	take over an airplane through violence
persuade	talk someone into doing something
valor	bravery

HEROES WHO BRAVED SNOW AND ICE

In 1925 many children in Nome, Alaska, were sick and dying. They would die if they did not get medicine quickly. But the medicine they needed was far away. The only way to get it to Nome was by dogsled.

A race to save lives

Each dogsled team raced to meet the next, passing on the medicine. It was like a **relay race**. In total, twenty dogsled teams traveled 674 miles (1,085 kilometers). They did this in five-and-a-half days. These human and dog heroes got the medicine to Nome. They saved hundreds of lives.

relay race | race in which each person races only part of the way, taking it in turns

The Iditarod race is held every year in Alaska to remember the heroes of 1925.

ALASKA

Nome

Nenana

Iditarod

N
W   E
S

0   50   100 Miles
0   50   100 Kilometers

Seward

---- 1925 Medicine route
—— Iditarod race route

Fascinating fact

The Iditarod dogsled race follows part of the path of the heroes.

LANCE ARMSTRONG

At age 25 Lance Armstrong was one of the world's best cyclists. Then, he found out he had cancer. He had two operations to treat the cancer.

A winner lives strong

After the operations, Armstrong was weak. Still, he had hope and courage. A few years later, Armstrong went on to win the Tour de France bicycle race seven times. "Before cancer, I just lived," he said. "Now I live strong."

Fascinating fact

Armstrong set up a charity. The Lance Armstrong Foundation raises money to help cancer patients.

| foundation | organization that helps those in need |

The Tour de France is a three-week-long bicycle race.

People wear wristbands to show they support Armstrong's charity.

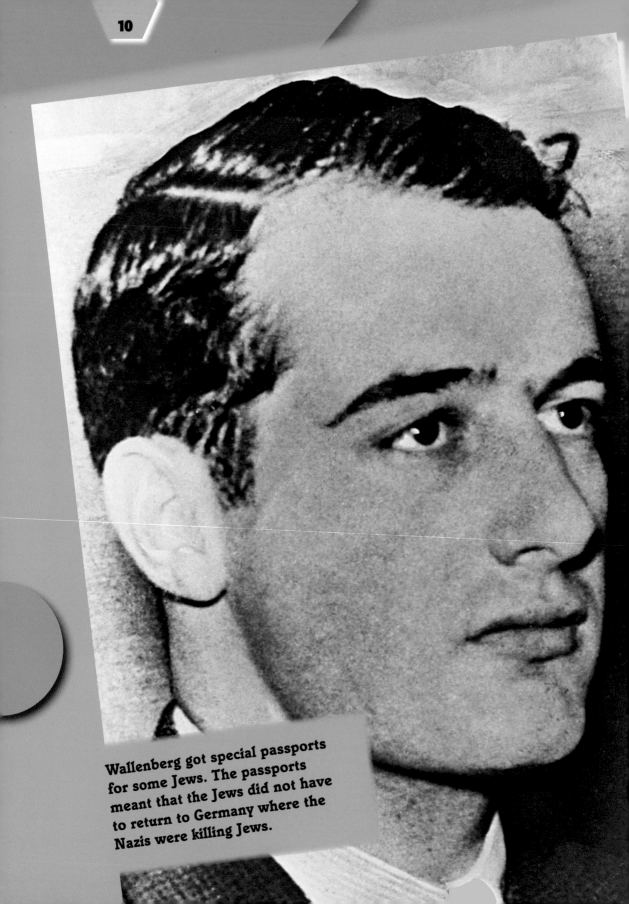

Wallenberg got special passports for some Jews. The passports meant that the Jews did not have to return to Germany where the Nazis were killing Jews.

HERO OF WORLD WAR II

In 1944 the **Nazis** in Germany were planning to kill 100,000 Jewish people. The Jews lived in a country called Hungary. Raoul Wallenberg found out about the plan.

Saving Jewish lives

Wallenberg helped many Jews hide. Then he told a Nazi general that killing the Jews would be a **war crime**. This scared the general. He called off the killings. In this way, Wallenberg saved more than 10,000 Jewish lives.

Fascinating fact

Wallenberg was arrested in 1945 because some people thought he was a spy. He has not been seen since.

Nazis	political party that controlled Germany from 1933 to 1945
war crime	crime committed during a war, such as killing people or treating prisoners very badly

HEROES OF SEPTEMBER 11

On September 11, 2001 a **terrorist** group called **al-Qaeda** flew planes into the World Trade Center in New York City. Terrorists attack and scare people. On this day, they killed thousands of people.

Just doing a job

People rushed out of the burning twin towers. As they left, firefighters ran into the buildings to help. Many people think firefighters are heroes. "We're just doing our jobs," said firefighter Kenny Haskell.

Kenny Haskell's two brothers were also firefighters. They died with many others when the twin towers collapsed.

al-Qaeda	group behind the September 11, 2001 attacks in the United States
terrorist	person who attacks and scares other people

Firefighters wanted to save lives on September 11. They had to go into dangerous areas.

Police rescue dogs
searched for survivors.

Rivera (center) said Salty's
actions were "amazing."

HEROIC DOGS OF SEPTEMBER 11

Omar Eduardo Rivera is blind. He was working in the World Trade Center when the planes hit.

A best friend

Rivera said, "I could hear how pieces of glass were flying around and falling. I could feel the smoke filling up my lungs."

Rivera has a **guide dog** called Salty. He set Salty free to escape the fires. However, Rivera said, "He returned to my side a few minutes later and guided me down 70 flights of stairs and out into the street."

Fascinating fact

A rescue dog helped locate a woman who was buried alive on September 11.

| guide dog | dog trained to help blind people |
| rescue dog | dog trained to find people |

People climbed onto roofs to be rescued by the helicopter team.

HEROES OF HURRICANE KATRINA

Hurricane Katrina was a deadly storm that hit in August 2005. The city of New Orleans, Louisiana, was flooded. Many people drowned. Others climbed as high as they could and waited for help.

Helicopter rescue

420 people were on the roof of a hotel. Michael Sorjonen was chief of a helicopter team. His team made nearly 30 difficult helicopter trips to rescue people. It took ten hours, but the rescue mission was a success. Everyone was saved.

hurricane	**powerful storm with strong winds and a lot of rain**

Reeve played Superman in the movies, but he was a hero in real life, too.

| paralyzed | not able to move parts of the body |

CHRISTOPHER REEVE

In 1995 "Superman" Christopher Reeve fell off a horse and broke his neck. He was **paralyzed**. He could not move below his neck or breathe without help from a machine.

A hero gives hope to others

At first doctors said Reeve would never improve, but he did not give up. "The only limits you have are those you put on yourself," he said. After a while he began to breathe on his own. He got some feeling back in one finger. This meant that he could use a wheelchair.

Reeve died in 2004. Thanks to him, doctors now have hope that paralyzed people can make progress.

Reeve never gave up hope.

SURFER HERO

Scott Larsen was surfing in Okinawa, Japan, when he saw a woman drowning. A strong tide had pulled her far from the beach.

Water rescue

First, Larsen helped her up onto his surfboard. Then he saw a man on a small raft who was in trouble too. So Larsen tied the raft to his surfboard. Then he paddled back to the beach with the woman on his surfboard, pulling the man on the raft.

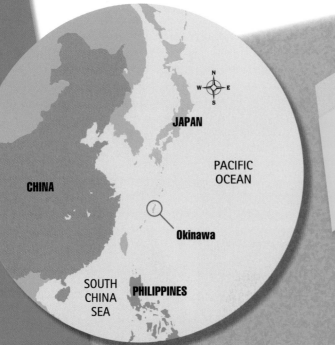

JAPAN

PACIFIC OCEAN

CHINA

Okinawa

SOUTH CHINA SEA

PHILIPPINES

Fascinating fact

Larsen is American. His family moved to Japan because of his parents' jobs.

Larsen used his surfing skills and his training as a lifeguard in his daring rescue.

The **thatched** roofs of the cottages were completely destroyed.

EDDIE YOUNG

One summer night in 2005 Eddie Young was driving in Oxford, England. He saw flames leaping from a row of houses.

Time to be a hero

At once Young stopped his car and ran into a burning house. He carried a 93-year-old woman out. Then he helped several other people escape the smoke and flames.

"If we were five minutes too early, we might not have seen the fire," Young said. "And if I didn't see it, these people might have all been dead."

Fascinating fact

In the U.S., house fire deaths have gone down by 50 percent. This is thanks to modern smoke detectors.

thatched | **roof covering of straw or reeds**

CAT HERO

In 1996 an old building in Brooklyn, New York, was on fire. A mother cat and her four-week-old kittens were caught inside.

A daring rescue

The mother cat was badly burned, but she did not give up on saving her kittens. A firefighter said, "She ran in and out of that building five times. She got them all out. Then she started moving the kittens one by one across the street."

Fascinating fact

The cat was named Scarlett because she had red, burned patches on her skin. Her fur soon grew back.

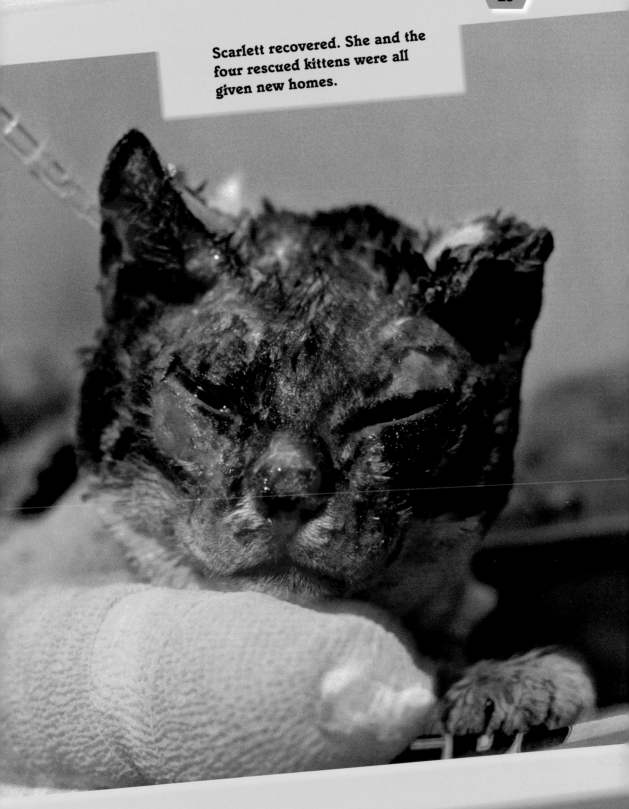

Scarlett recovered. She and the four rescued kittens were all given new homes.

Lulu is an eastern gray kangaroo like this one.

KANGAROO HERO

In 2003 Australian farmer Len Richards was knocked **unconscious** by a tree branch. No one knew he was hurt, except his pet kangaroo named Lulu.

Lulu to the rescue

Lulu "barked like a dog," said Len's daughter Celeste. "She was obviously trying to get our attention because she never acts like that."

Thanks to Lulu, the family found Len. "If it wasn't for her, my dad could have died," Celeste said. "Lulu is my hero."

Fascinating fact

Lulu became famous. She appeared on TV shows in Australia.

unconscious   knocked out, not awake

GREAT HEROES

All the heroes in this book were brave. They took risks to help others. They did not give up.

Free The Children

In 1995 twelve-year-old Craig Kielburger started an organization called Free The Children. Craig is from Toronto, Canada. He read about a boy of his age in Pakistan. The boy was killed for complaining about the way children in Pakistan were forced to work. Craig thought the boy was a hero, because he had given his life to help his friends.

Craig said, "I suddenly understood that a young person can make a difference." So he set up Free The Children to help young people around the world.

Fascinating fact

Free The Children youth volunteers raise money. They have raised enough to build 430 schools in 21 countries.

Craig spends his life helping children in many countries.

Glossary

al-Qaeda group behind the September 11, 2001, attacks in the United States

foundation organization that helps those in need

guide dog dog trained to help blind people

hijack take over an airplane through violence

hurricane powerful storm with strong winds and a lot of rain

Nazi political party that controlled Germany from 1933 to 1945. Adolf Hitler led this party during World War II.

paralyzed not able to move parts of the body

persuade talk someone into doing something

relay race race in which each person races only part of the way, taking it in turns

rescue dog dog trained to find people

terrorist person who attacks and scares other people

thatched roof covering of straw or reeds

unconscious knocked out, not awake

valor bravery

war crime crime committed during a war, such as killing people or treating prisoners very badly

Want to Know More?

Books

✳ Abraham, Philip. *Christopher Reeve* New York: Children's Press, 2002.

✳ Denenberg, Dennis, and Lorraine Roscoe. *50 American Heroes Every Kid Should Meet.* Brookfield, Conn.: Millbrook, 2001.

✳ Jackson, Donna M. *Hero Dogs: Courageous Canines in Action.* New York: Little, Brown, 2003.

✳ Miller, Debbie S. *The Great Serum Race: Blazing the Iditarod Trail.* New York: Walker and Co., 2002.

Websites

✳ www.freethechildren.org
Read about Free The Children. You could become a volunteer.

✳ www.myhero.com
Find out about heroes, from animals to scientists. Talk about your own heroes.

✳ www.rolemodel.net
Search through details of celebrities who have helped others.

If you liked this Atomic book, why don't you try these...?

Index